ICE HOCKEY

THIS EDITION
Produced for DK by WonderLab Group LLC
Jennifer Emmett, Erica Green, Kate Hale, *Founders*

Editor Maya Myers; **Photography Editor** Nicole DiMella; **Managing Editor** Rachel Houghton;
Designers Project Design Company; **Researcher** Michelle Harris; **Copy Editor** Lori Merritt;
Indexer Connie Binder; **Proofreader** Susan K. Hom; **Series Reading Specialist** Dr. Jennifer Albro

First American Edition, 2025
Published in the United States by DK Publishing, a division of Penguin Random House LLC
1745 Broadway, 20th Floor, New York, NY 10019

Copyright © 2025 Dorling Kindersley Limited
24 25 26 27 10 9 8 7 6 5 4 3 2 1
001-345672-June/2025

All rights reserved.
Without limiting the rights under the copyright reserved above, no part of this publication may be reproduced, stored in or introduced into a retrieval system, or transmitted, in any form, or by any means (electronic, mechanical, photocopying, recording, or otherwise), without the prior written permission of the copyright owner.
Published in Great Britain by Dorling Kindersley Limited

A catalog record for this book is available from the Library of Congress.
HC ISBN: 978-0-5939-6619-8
PB ISBN: 978-0-5939-6618-1

DK books are available at special discounts when purchased in bulk for sales promotions, premiums, fund-raising, or educational use.
For details, contact:
DK Publishing Special Markets, 1745 Broadway, 20th Floor, New York, NY 10019
SpecialSales@dk.com

Printed and bound in China
Super Readers Lexile® levels 620L to 790L
Lexile® is the registered trademark of MetaMetrics, Inc. Copyright © 2024 MetaMetrics, Inc. All rights reserved.

The publisher would like to thank the following for their kind permission to reproduce their images:
a=above; c=centre; b=below; l=left; r=right; t=top; b/g=background
Alamy Stock Photo: Abaca Press / Gouhier-Zabulon 3, Cal Sport Media 6, Cal Sport Media / Burt Granofsky 7t, 13t, 31tr, Cal Sport Media / Jonathan Tenca 20t, CTK / David Tanecek 22, Karl Denham 12br, Luke Durda 21, Colin Edwards 14t, EMU history 11br, IanDagnall Computing 9bc, Imago 45t, Les Archives Digitales 9tr, Andy Martin Jr 26, Mpi04 / Media Punch 43tr, NTB / Johnny Syversen 29cla, UPI / Kevin Dietsch 29cra, UPI / Mark Goldman 36t, Zuma Press, Inc. / John Rowland / Southcreek 27t; **Dreamstime.com:** Oleg Dudko 17br, Enterlinedesign 13b, Mariakray 30-31 (Background), 38-39 (Background), Volodymyr Melnyk 16, Alexander Mosiychuk 14cr, Nikita Rublev 17tr, 17cla, 17cr, 17bl, Mohamed Ahmed Soliman 19clb, Julia Sudnitskaya 28-29 (Background), 34-35 (Background), 40-41 (Background), Trotzolga12 32-33 (Background), 36-37 (Background); **Getty Images:** Graig Abel 29cl, Archive Photos / FPG 40t, Brian Bahr 38b, Bruce Bennett 30cr, 33t, 40b, 45cra, Bruce Bennett / C Andersen 29clb, Bruce Bennett / R Laberge 28b, Bettmann 29cra (Gordie Howe), 30b, 32cra, Steph Chambers 15, Collection Mix: Subjects / Caia Image 4-5, Steve Crandall 29cr, Jonathan Daniel 41t, De Agostini / Dea / G. Dagli Orti 8, DigitalVision / LWA / Dann Tardif 7b, Elsa 1, Focus On Sport 23b, 39t, Hulton Archive 9crb, Hulton Archive / Print Collector 11t, 23t, Icon Sportswire 20b, Alex Livesey 35b, Ethan Miller 37b, National Hockey League / Brian Babineau 41cr, National Hockey League / Dave Sandford 19cr, National Hockey League / Jeff Vinnick 44, National Hockey League / Minas Panagiotakis 45b, National Hockey League / Steve Babineau 29bc, 39b, New York Daily News 18, 32bl, Doug Pensinger 25b, Robert Riger 34, Rick Stewart 35t, Toronto Star / John Mahler 27b, Tribune News Service / MCT 25t, 31cr, Visual China Group 24; **Library of Congress, Washington, D.C.:** 11tr, 11cl; **Shutterstock.com:** Meunierd 42, Pikovit 13br, SeventyFour 12clb

Cover images: *Front:* **Alamy Stock Photo:** Kirby Lee cra, UPI / Bill Greenblatt cla, ZUMA Press, Inc. / Alex Cave, ZUMA Press, Inc. / Spencer Lee c; **Getty Images:** Icon Sportswire cl; *Back:* **Dreamstime.com:** Sfanats cl; **Getty Images / iStock:** Elena Istomina cla; **Shutterstock.com:** Robinart cra

www.dk.com

This book was made with Forest Stewardship Council™ certified paper – one small step in DK's commitment to a sustainable future.
Learn more at www.dk.com/uk/information/sustainability

Level 3

Ice Hockey

Eric Zweig

Contents

- **6** Hockey Today
- **8** Early Hockey History
- **10** Modern Hockey
- **12** Let's Play!
- **14** On the Ice
- **16** Getting in Gear
- **18** The National Hockey League
- **20** Other Leagues
- **22** International Hockey

26	Super Scorers
32	Great Goalies
38	Dominant Defenders
42	The Stanley Cup Story
44	The Future of Hockey
46	Glossary
47	Index
48	Quiz

Hockey Today

Slap! The stick smacks the puck and shoots it across the ice. It speeds past the goalie and into the net. Score!

People think of ice hockey as a winter game. It's played on a frozen ice rink. When people first started playing hockey, they played it only during the winter. These days, the hockey season begins as early as September. It can stretch well into June. In the Northern Hemisphere, that's fall, winter, spring, and a bit of summer, too!

Rieger Lorenz

The Minnesota Frost, 2024

The best men's hockey players from around the world play in the National Hockey League, called the NHL for short. The top women's players play in the Professional Women's Hockey League, or the PWHL. Both leagues have teams based in Canada and the US.

Kids all around the world play hockey, too! Boys and girls can start playing youth hockey around the age of six. When they get older, they can move up to junior hockey. Some people play hockey at their college or university.

Ancient Greek depiction of hockey, 5th century BCE

Early Hockey History

When did people first play hockey? Where did they first play it? Nobody knows for sure!

Drawings and carvings from ancient Egypt and Greece show people playing games like hockey thousands of years ago. But those games weren't played on ice. They were more like field hockey.

In Ireland and Scotland, people played field sports called hurling and shinty. These sports also have ancient roots. They became very popular in the 1800s. The women's version of hurling is camogie. Hurling and camogie are still popular in Ireland.

1864 illustration of a field hockey stick

In Holland in the 1500s, people played a game that looked like golf on ice. In England, Russia, Sweden, and other countries, people in the 1800s played a skating game called bandy. (It's still popular in Russia and Sweden.) When people from Europe first came to North America, they saw Indigenous people playing lacrosse on ice in the winter.

All these games helped inspire ice hockey as we know it today.

9

Modern Hockey

Early ice hockey was played outdoors on frozen lakes and rivers. The first official indoor hockey game took place in the Canadian city of Montreal on March 3, 1875. Many people consider that game to be the start of modern hockey.

Soon, people were playing hockey all across Canada. It became popular in the northern and eastern parts of the US, too. A group of teams formed the first official hockey league in Montreal during the winter months of 1886 and 1887. The NHL started in December 1917.

Women's hockey was very popular at that time, too. However, not everyone supported girls and women playing hockey. Many people thought the game was too rough for them. The launch of a new professional women's league in 2024 marked a new era for women's hockey.

St. Moritz, Switzerland

New York amateur league champs, 1911

Playing for fun in Massachusetts, 1912

Moving Indoors
Early indoor hockey games in Montreal were played at the Victoria Skating Rink. The Montreal Arena opened in 1898. It was the first ice rink built especially for hockey games.

Let's Play!

Hockey is one of the fastest sports on Earth. Because the game is played wearing skates on ice, players move much faster than people can run on a field or a floor. Hockey players use their sticks to shoot the puck close to 100 miles per hour (160 km/h)! You need fast reflexes to stop those shots!

The main object in hockey is to shoot the puck into the other team's net. This is called scoring a goal. The team that scores the most goals wins the game.

Hockey today has six positions on the ice. There's a center, a left winger, and a right winger. Those players are known as forwards. Their main job is to score goals. There are also two defensive players. Their main job is to help the sixth player, the goalie, stop the other team from scoring.

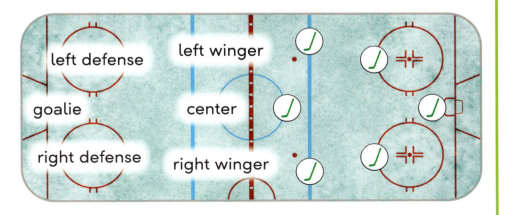

On the Ice

A hockey rink has a red line across the middle. Two blue lines split the ice into three zones. Players can move the puck by skating with it, or by passing it forward or backward. However, the puck must always cross the blue line into the other team's zone before a player does.

Officials watch to make sure the rules are followed. These are the referees and linesmen or lineswomen. When a player on the ice does something that's against the rules, the referee can call a penalty. A penalty removes the player from the ice for a few minutes.

The red circles on the ice are used for face-offs. A face-off is when a referee drops the puck onto the ice between two players to start the action.

First Female Coach

Jessica Campbell is the first woman to serve as an on-bench NHL assistant coach. She coaches for the Seattle Kraken. She played at Cornell University. She also played in the old Canadian Women's Hockey League.

Getting in Gear

Hockey is a physically demanding game. It's played on a hard, slippery surface. Players can bang into the player who has the puck. This is called bodychecking. Players may crash into the boards around the ice. Proper protection is important to keep players safe.

Heads Up
Today, we know that head injuries can cause serious damage to the brain. But hockey players haven't always protected their heads very well. Most goalies didn't wear masks on their faces until the 1960s. Helmets became popular around that time, too.

Hockey players wear gloves. They have pads to protect their knees and shins, wrists, elbows, and shoulders. There's equipment to protect their private parts, too. Goalies wear large pads on their legs and use special gloves. And all players wear helmets with face shields.

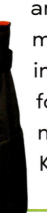

Hockey equipment used to be made from materials like felt, leather, wood, and plastic. It could be very heavy. Today, hockey equipment is stronger and lighter. It is made from modern materials, including foam rubber, nylon, and Kevlar.

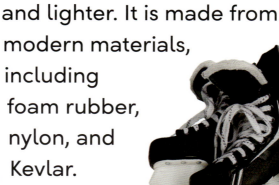

The National Hockey League

When the NHL started in 1917, it had only four teams. (One of them went out of business before the season ended!) Today, the NHL has 32 teams. They play all across North America, in the east, west, north, and south. There are seven NHL teams in Canada, and 25 in the US.

The New York Rangers receiving the Stanley Cup, 1933

NHL teams play in two conferences: the Eastern Conference and the Western Conference. Each conference has 16 teams. The conferences are split into two divisions of eight teams.

A team plays 82 games in a season. At the end of the regular season, just 16 teams make the playoffs. At the end of the playoffs, the champion wins the Stanley Cup.

The Florida Panthers after winning the Stanley Cup in 2024

The Original Six

For 25 seasons, from 1942 until 1967, the NHL had six teams. Today, those teams are known as The Original Six. They are the Montreal Canadiens, the Toronto Maple Leafs, the Boston Bruins, the New York Rangers, the Detroit Red Wings, and the Chicago Blackhawks.

Other Leagues

American Hockey League (AHL)

Michael Mersch, Jordy Bellerive

This league is one step below the NHL. Many young players who aren't ready for the NHL hope to improve their skills by playing in the AHL.

National Collegiate Athletic Association (NCAA)

The NCAA is an organization of sports at American universities and colleges. NCAA hockey is a way for players to try to earn a spot in the NHL while getting an education. The NCAA is a particularly important training ground for women's players.

Loren Gabel, Presley Norby

Canadian Hockey League (CHL)

This organization runs three different junior hockey leagues. They are the Ontario Hockey League, the Western Hockey League, and the Quebec Maritimes Junior Hockey League. Some junior teams in these three leagues are based in American cities. In Canada, junior hockey is the most common way for young players to try to make the NHL.

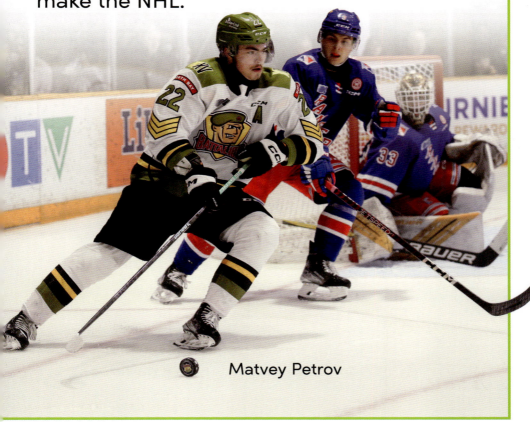

Matvey Petrov

International Hockey

The International Ice Hockey Federation dates back to 1908. Today, 83 countries are members.

Many countries in Europe have their own hockey leagues. The best leagues are in Sweden, Finland, Czechia, Germany, Switzerland, and Russia. The best hockey players from Europe often come to North America to play in the NHL and the PWHL.

USA playing Czech Republic in a World Championship quarter-final game, 2023

Great Britain's gold medal–winning Olympic team, 1936

It's exciting when the world's best hockey players get to represent their own countries in international competitions. Men's hockey has been part of the Winter Olympics since 1924. Hockey was even part of the Summer Olympics in 1920.

Miracle on Ice

Professional athletes couldn't play in the Winter Olympics until 1988. In 1980, the US hockey team was mostly made up of college players. The powerful Soviet Olympic team almost never lost. When the US beat the Soviet Union, it was a big surprise! Some people called it "the Miracle on Ice."

Hayley Scamurra (US) and Jocelyne Larocque (Canada) during the gold-medal game at the 2022 Olympics

There has been a Women's World Championship since 1990. Canada dominated the early World Championships. They won eight straight gold medals. Women's hockey has been a Winter Olympics event since 1998. The United States won the first Olympic gold medal at the 1998 Winter Games. The rivalry between the women's hockey teams from Canada and the US is one of the fiercest in all of sports!

Hayley Wickenheiser

Canadian Hayley Wickenheiser is the top scorer in Olympic hockey history. She went to the Olympics five times and played in 26 games. She scored 18 goals and had 33 assists. Wickenheiser won four gold medals and one silver. At 13 Women's World Championships, she won seven golds and six silvers. Wickenheiser played for 23 years with the Canadian women's national team. Many people consider her the greatest women's hockey player of all time.

Super Scorers

The top scorers in hockey almost always play at a forward position. Many forwards are great at shooting the puck. Some are so quick that they catch goalies by surprise. Some have a powerful shot that's hard to stop. Other forwards are great at passing the puck. They set their teammates up to score goals.

Alex Ovechkin

Players score goals for their team. At the same time, they are collecting individual points. Every goal a player scores is worth one point. Players also get a point if they help a teammate score a goal. That's called an assist. The total of a player's goals and assists equals their total points. All these numbers are tracked for every player. Points are totaled for each season. The player who leads the NHL in points each season wins the Art Ross Trophy. Points are also totaled for a player's entire career.

Jarome Iginla

Wayne Gretzky

Wayne Gretzky

Wayne Gretzky was a star center in the NHL from 1979 to 1999. He played for the Edmonton Oilers, the Los Angeles Kings, the St. Louis Blues, and the New York Rangers. People call him "the Great One." He was excellent at anticipating what would happen next on the ice. Gretzky set 61 records during his career. He scored a record 92 goals in a single season in 1981–82. He also set the single-season record for assists (163) and points (215) in 1985–86. Gretzky won the Art Ross Trophy a record 10 times in his career. He won the Hart Memorial Trophy nine times. That trophy goes to the NHL's most valuable player.

NHL Leaders in Goals
(Through the 2023–2024 Season)

Single Season		Career	
Wayne Gretzky, Edmonton (1981–1982)	92	Wayne Gretzky (1979–1999)	894
Wayne Gretzky, Edmonton (1983–1984)	87	Alex Ovechkin* (2005–2024)	853
Brett Hull, St. Louis (1990–1991)	86	Gordie Howe (1946–1980)	801
Mario Lemieux, Pittsburgh (1988–1989)	85	Jaromír Jágr (1990–2018)	766
Phil Esposito, Boston (1970–1971)	76	Brett Hull (1986–2006)	741
Alexander Mogilny, Buffalo (1992–1993)	76	*Still active	
Teemu Selänne, Winnipeg (1992–1993)	76		

Maurice Richard

Maurice Richard played right wing for the Montreal Canadiens from 1942 until 1960. He was known as "the Rocket." He had explosive speed and scoring power. Richard was the first NHL player to score 50 goals in one season. He was also the first to score 500 goals in his career. Today, the player who leads the NHL in goals each year wins the Rocket Richard Trophy.

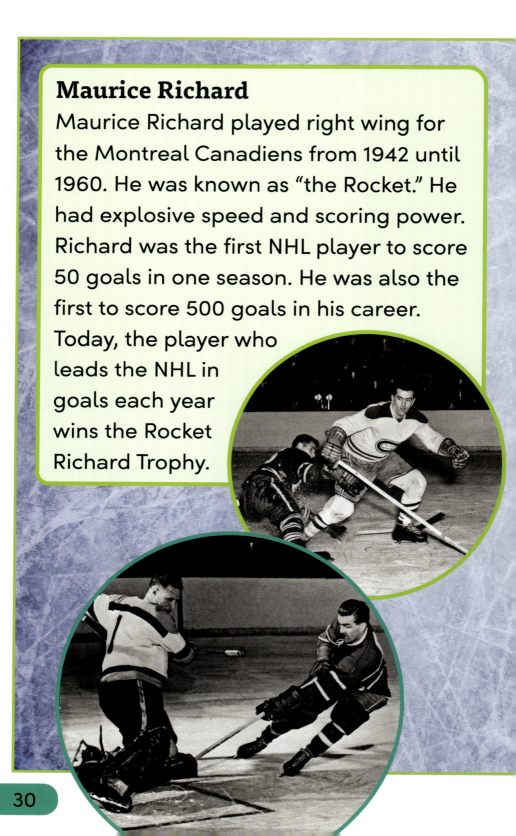

Hilary Knight

American forward Hilary Knight has the most goals of any player in the history of the Women's World Championships. As of 2024, she has scored 65 goals in 80 games. Knight has also won the most medals at the Women's World Championship: nine golds and five silvers.

Marie-Philip Poulin

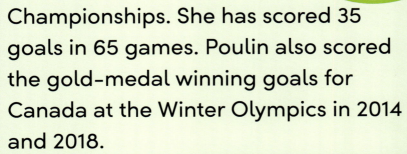

Among active players, Canada's Marie-Philip Poulin is second in goals at the Women's World Championships. She has scored 35 goals in 65 games. Poulin also scored the gold-medal winning goals for Canada at the Winter Olympics in 2014 and 2018.

Great Goalies

The team that scores the most goals wins the game. So, preventing the other team from scoring is important! A goalie can use any part of their body to stop the puck.

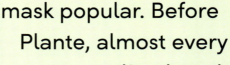

Jacques Plante

Jacques Plante is one of the most famous goalies in hockey history. He starred in the NHL from 1952 to 1973. Plante won the Vezina Trophy a record seven times. He also made the goalie mask popular. Before Plante, almost every goalie played with a bare face. It was very dangerous!

Connor Hellebuyck

Vezina Trophy

The player who is voted the NHL's best goalie each season wins the Vezina Trophy. The trophy is named after Georges Vezina, who was a star with the Montreal Canadiens.

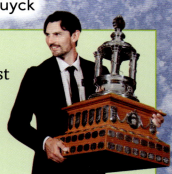

Recent Winners

Connor Hellebuyck, Winnipeg Jets	2024
Linus Ullmark, Boston Bruins	2023
Igor Shesterkin, New York Rangers	2022
Marc-André Fleury, Vegas Golden Knights	2021
Connor Hellebuyck, Winnipeg Jets	2020

Terry Sawchuk

Who is hockey's greatest goalie? Many people think it's Terry Sawchuk. He played 21 seasons between 1950 and 1970. He had 445 wins and 103 shutouts. A shutout is when the goalie keeps the other team from scoring any goals in a game. For years, this was the most in NHL history. Before Sawchuk, goalies usually tried to keep their unmasked faces far from the puck. But Sawchuk played crouching low on the ice. Today, all goalies play low like he did.

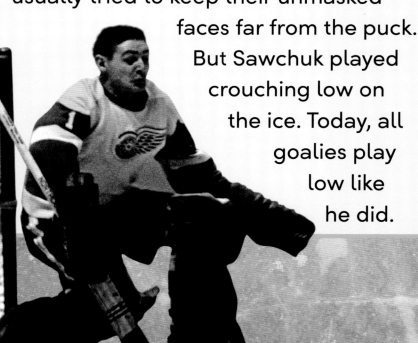

Dominik Hašek

Dominik Hašek was the greatest goalie in the 1990s and early 2000s. Hašek had an unusual style. He would twist and flop on the ice. But he always seemed to stop the puck. He played with the Buffalo Sabres from 1992 to 2001. Hašek won the Vezina Trophy six times while he was playing with the Sabres.

Hall of Fame

The game's greatest players are honored in the Hockey Hall of Fame. In 2020, Kim St-Pierre became the first female goalie in the Hall of Fame. Canada won three Olympic gold medals and five World Championships with St-Pierre in the goal.

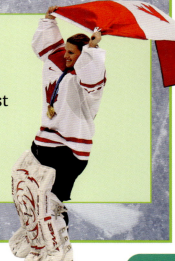

By the numbers, Martin Brodeur is the all-time best goalie. Here are the top five NHL leaders in career wins and career shutouts through the 2023–24 season.

Wins		Shutouts	
Martin Brodeur (1991–2015)	691	Martin Brodeur (1991–2015)	125
Marc-André Fleury* (2004–2024)	561	Terry Sawchuk (1949–1970)	103
Patrick Roy (1984–2003)	551	George Hainsworth (1926–1937)	94
Roberto Luongo (1999–2019)	489	Glenn Hall (1952–1971)	84
Ed Belfour (1988–2007)	484	Jacques Plante (1952–1973)	82

*Still active

Goalie MVPs

Only seven goalies have won the Hart Trophy for the NHL's most valuable player.

Roy Worters, New York Americans	1928–1929
Chuck Rayner, New York Rangers	1949–1950
Al Rollins, Chicgo Blackhawks	1953–1954
Jacques Plante, Montreal Canadiens	1961–1962
Dominik Hašek, Buffalo Sabres	1996–1997
Dominik Hašek, Buffalo Sabres	1997–1998
José Théodore, Montreal Canadiens	2001–2002
Carey Price, Montreal Canadiens	2014–2015

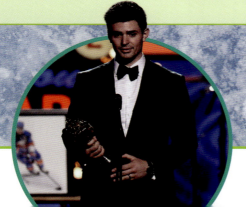

Carey Price

Dominant Defenders

When the other team has the puck, your team is playing defense. A defender's job is to get the puck out of their end of the ice. It helps to be strong and fast. Defenders who can also help their forwards score are very valuable players.

Geraldine Heaney

Geraldine Heaney's skill with the puck revolutionized women's hockey. She helped Canada win gold medals at the first seven Women's World Championships. Heaney also played with the semi-professional Toronto Aeros. They won six Canadian provincial championships in Ontario during her 18 years with the team.

Bobby Orr

Bobby Orr was the biggest star in hockey in the 1960s and '70s. He played for the Boston Bruins. Many people think he's the greatest player of all time. Orr had blazing speed. He was great at moving the puck out of his end. He was also amazing on offense. Orr is the only defender to lead the NHL in scoring. And he did it twice! He also won the Norris Trophy, for the NHL's best defender, a record eight times. Sadly, knee injuries cut his career short.

Eddie Shore

Eddie Shore was a star for the Boston Bruins from 1926 to 1939. Like Bobby Orr, Shore was a powerful skater. Shore is the only defender in NHL history to win the Hart Trophy as MVP four times. Orr won it three times. Only five other defenders have even won it once.

Doug Harvey

Doug Harvey was an NHL star from 1947 to 1969. He won the Norris Trophy seven times. Harvey was extremely good on defense. People said he controlled the pace of every player on the ice.

Nicklas Lidström

Nicklas Lidström starred with the Detroit Red Wings from 1991 to 2012. Lidström always seemed to know where to be. That's how he kept his opponents under control. Like Harvey, Lidström won the Norris Trophy seven times.

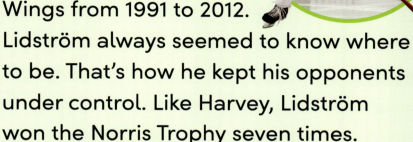

Quinn Hughes

Defense!
Recent winners of the Norris Trophy:

Quinn Hughes, Vancouver Canucks	2024
Erik Karlsson, San Jose Sharks	2023
Cale Makar, Colorado Avalanche	2022
Adam Fox, New York Rangers	2021
Roman Josi, Nashville Predators	2020

The Stanley Cup Story

The Stanley Cup is the oldest professional sports trophy in North America. It's awarded each year to the champions of the NHL. But the Stanley Cup is older than the NHL. It was first presented in 1893. The Montreal Canadiens have won the Stanley Cup a record 24 times.

Originally, the Stanley Cup was the size of the bowl that tops the trophy today. The name of the winning team and its players are engraved onto a band on the base of the trophy. As the Stanley Cup got bigger, its shape changed, too. Now, when a new band gets added, an old one is removed.

The Stanley Cup

The Stanley Cup is named after Lord Stanley, the Governor-General of Canada from 1888 to 1893.

Most Stanley Cup Wins		Recent Stanley Cup Wins	
Montreal Canadiens (1917–2024)	24*	Florida Panthers	2024
Toronto Maple Leafs (1917–2024)	13°	Vegas Golden Knights	2023
Detroit Red Wings (1926–2024)	11	Colorado Avalanche	2022
Boston Bruins (1924–2024)	6	Tampa Bay Lightning	2021
Chicago Blackhawks (1926–2024)	6	Tampa Bay Lightning	2020
Edmonton Oilers (1979–2024) Pittsburgh Penguins (1967–2024)	5	St. Louis Blues	2019

*Won for the first time in 1916, before the NHL was formed
° Includes Toronto Arenas (1918); Toronto St. Patricks (1922)

The Future of Hockey

The future of hockey may involve new technology. Hockey equipment could add sensors to check a player's skill or health. New technology could help ice rinks become more energy efficient.

On the ice, the NHL may add more teams. The PWHL certainly will. The women's league began with six teams playing 24 games each in 2023–24. Both the number of games and the number of teams will grow in coming years. Hockey fans are looking forward to the return of NHL players to the Winter Olympics. For various reasons, the NHL missed the Games in 2018 and 2022. But they will be back for the Olympics in 2026 and 2030.

In women's hockey, all the Olympic gold medals have been won by Canada or the United States. But women's hockey is growing more popular everywhere. So, another team may someday win the Women's World Championship or an Olympic gold medal.

Keep your head up when you're on the ice to see what's coming!

Glossary

Arena
A building with seats inside where people can watch sports or other entertainment

Assist
A play that helps a teammate score a goal

Bodycheck
Using your body to bump into an opponent who has the puck

Championship
A contest to determine an overall winner

Conference
A larger group of sports teams that play together in a league

Division
A smaller group of sports teams that play together in a league, often within a conference

Equipment
Items needed for a particular purpose, such as playing a sport

Goal
A score in hockey, earned when a player puts the puck into the other team's net

League
A group of sports teams that play together

Modern
Happening in the present day or recent past

Playoffs
A tournament at the end of the regular season to determine an overall winner

Point
Hockey players earn one point for every goal they score and every assist they make

Professional
A person who gets paid to do something

Puck
A hard, flat, rubber object (usually black) used to play hockey

Reflexes
The body's automatic responses to stimuli

Rink
A large, flat area often with ice for skating; a building that contains such an area

Rivalry
An ongoing competition between two teams, over the course of many games

Skates
Boots with sharp blades attached to the bottom, for moving quickly on ice

Zone
A specific area on a hockey rink

Index

American Hockey League (AHL) 20
assists 27, 28
Belfour, Ed 36
Brodeur, Martin 36
Campbell, Jessica 15
Canadian Hockey League (CHL) 21
defenders 13, 38–41
equipment 16–17, 32, 44
Esposito, Phil 29
Fleury, Marc-André 33, 36
forwards 13, 26, 38
Fox, Adam 41
future of hockey 44–45
gear 16–17, 32, 44
goalies 13, 16, 26, 32–37
goals, scoring 12, 13, 26–31
Gretzky, Wayne 27, 28, 29
Hainsworth, George 36
Hall, Glenn 36
Harvey, Doug 40, 41
Hašek, Dominik 35, 37
Heaney, Geraldine 38
Hellebuyck, Connor 33
history of hockey 8–9, 18, 19, 42
Howe, Gordie 29
Hughes, Quinn 41
Hull, Brett 29
international hockey 8–9, 22–23, 45

Jágr, Jaromír 29
Josi, Roman 41
junior hockey 7, 21
Karlsson, Erik 41
Knight, Hilary 31
Lemieux, Mario 29
Lidström, Nicklas 41
Luongo, Roberto 36
Makar, Cale 41
Mogilny, Alexander 29
National Collegiate Athletic Association (NCAA) 20
National Hockey League (NHL)
  female coach 15
  future 44
  great defenders 39–41
  great goalies 32–37
  great scorers 26–31, 39
  history 10, 18
  international players 7, 22
  Olympics 44
  teams and conferences 18–19
Olympics 23, 24, 25, 31, 35, 44–45
Orr, Bobby 39, 40
Ovechkin, Alex 26, 29
Plante, Jacques 32, 36, 37
Poulin, Marie-Philip 31
Price, Carey 37

Professional Women's Hockey League (PWHL) 7, 22, 44
Rayner, Chuck 37
Richard, Maurice 30
rink 14, 15, 44
Rollins, Al 37
Roy, Patrick 36
Sawchuk, Terry 34, 36
Selänne, Teemu 29
Shesterkin, Igor 33
Shore, Eddie 40
Stanley, Lord 43
Stanley Cup 18, 19, 42–43
St-Pierre, Kim 35
Thédore, José 37
Ullmark, Linus 33
Vezina, Georges 33
Wickenheiser, Hayley 25
women
  coaches 15
  future of hockey 44, 45
  great players 25, 31, 35, 38
  leagues 7, 10, 15, 20, 44
  Olympics 24, 25, 31, 35, 45
  World Championships 24, 25, 31, 35, 38, 45
Worters, Roy 37
youth hockey 7

Quiz

Answer the questions to see what you have learned. Check your answers in the key below.

1. Which three positions on a hockey team are known as the forwards?
2. Name one of the early games that may have helped to inspire ice hockey?
3. How many teams are in the NHL today?
4. What is Wayne Gretzky's single-season record for most goals?
5. Who is the all-time leading scorer at the Women's World Championships?

1. Center, left wing, right wing 2. Shinty, hurling, bandy, or lacrosse on ice 3. 32 4. 92 5. Hilary Knight